YOU CHOOSE

CAN YOU SURVIVE A SURGING TSUNAMI?

An Interactive Survival Adventure

by Matt Doeden

CAPSTONE PRESS
a capstone imprint

Published by Capstone Press, an imprint of Capstone
1710 Roe Crest Drive, North Mankato, Minnesota 56003
capstonepub.com

Library of Congress Cataloging-in-Publication Data is available on the Library of Congress website.
ISBN: 9798875240645 (hardcover)
ISBN: 9798875240614 (paperback)
ISBN: 9798875240621 (ebook PDF)

Summary: You Choose lets YOU control the story! Readers choose their own paths while encountering a tsunami in three different scenarios. The outcomes are different as decisions are made throughout the book.

Editorial Credits
Editor: Mandy Robbins; Designer: Heidi Thompson; Media Researcher: Rebekah Hubstenberger; Production Specialist: Tori Abraham

Image Credits
Getty Images: 103, Ulet Ifansasti, 105; Shutterstock: ABCDstock, 26, Andrey Muravin, 16, ARTpok, 90, Dariush M, 28, Designua, 99, Emvat Mosakovskis, 20, FamVeld, 13, FOTOKITA, cover, GLBG, 23, Krasula, 53, Max666007, 78, Maximillian cabinet, 37, mTaira, 104, New Africa, 107, Nikola Fific, 93, Nixx Photography, 55, photka, 109, Rocksweeper, 60, T. Shahrizal Thajeb, 32, terekhov igor, 49, Wiparat P (texture background), back cover and throughout, Zorro Stock Images, 72

Printed and bound in China. 006461

TABLE OF CONTENTS

INTRODUCTION

ABOUT YOUR ADVENTURE

YOU are there when the chaos strikes along the coast. The ground shakes. Miles away, an earthquake has jolted the seafloor. A giant wave—a tsunami—is on its way. Where will you go? Will you save yourself or risk your life to save others? Your choices guide the story as this natural disaster unravels all around you. Will you live or die? Turn the page to find out.

Chapter One sets the scene. Then you choose which path to read. Follow the directions at the bottom of the page. Your decisions will change your outcome. After you finish one path, go back and read the others for new perspectives and more adventures.

Turn the page to begin your adventure.

CHAPTER 1

EARTHSHAKING

The sun shines bright and hot on your skin. As you gaze out over the endless blue horizon, the ground under your feet suddenly begins to rumble and shake.

"Whoa," you blurt out.

You throw your hands out to your sides to help steady your balance. Around you, other people are doing the same. One old man is crouching down covering his head with his arms.

You've lived through earthquakes before, but this one feels a bit stronger than you're used to. It goes on for a few more seconds before the ground once again feels solid beneath your feet.

Turn the page.

"That was a big one, eh?" the old man calls to you, a nervous grin on his face.

You smile back. "Yeah, had to be at least a six on the Richter scale, I'd guess."

The old man shakes his head and dismisses you with a wave of his hand. "Nonsense. That was a seven if ever I felt one. Well, I guess it's over now. Best be on my way home. Keep your eyes on the ocean."

That's when a siren begins to wail. You look to the sky for signs of bad weather, but it's clear blue. You cast your gaze along the coastline. Most people are rushing away from the water—while a few curious folks seem to be hurrying straight toward it. A woman runs past you with a baby in her arms. A young couple is pointing toward the shore. A tsunami is on its way.

To be a tourist walking your dog, turn to page 11.

To be a young fisherman, turn to page 45.

To try to help as a police rescue pilot, turn to page 71.

WHAT IS A TSUNAMI?

Tsunamis are huge waves caused by earthquakes or volcanoes on the ocean floor. In deep water, they are barely noticeable. But in shallow coastal areas, they swell. They can rush onto land with terrible power. On average, Earth has about two damage-causing tsunamis per year. Any coastal area can be at risk. But coasts along the Pacific Ocean and Indian Ocean are at the highest risk. Those areas tend to be the most active with earthquakes and volcanoes.

CHAPTER 2

NO DAY AT THE BEACH

This was supposed to be a relaxing afternoon. It's just you and Max, your terrier, out for a walk along the beach. But now, there's panic and confusion everywhere. A siren continues to wail in the distance. People scatter in every direction. Max tugs on his leash. He lets out a few small yips.

"What's wrong, Max?" you ask him.

You've trained him well. He rarely barks and never pulls on his leash when you're walking him. But something clearly has the little dog on edge. Perhaps the siren is hurting his ears.

You kneel down and pet him. You can feel his whole body shaking.

Turn the page.

"Is the siren really that bad?"

You should probably take him back to the little house along the coast that you are renting for the summer. It's just a ten-minute walk from here. But as you look at the beach, you see that the water doesn't meet the land in the usual spot. It's much farther back. Rocks and sand that should be covered by a foot of water are suddenly visible. You want to investigate.

"Come on, boy, let's check this out," you say, giving a gentle tug on the leash.

Max doesn't budge. He just stares out at the ocean. His tail is usually wagging when you're out on a walk. But now it's tucked down.

"Max, come on," you say a bit more firmly.

You give the leash another tug. This time, he reluctantly follows you.

A few concrete stairs lead down to a sandy beach. As you start down them, a woman carrying a beach towel brushes past you.

"You're going the wrong way," she says. "That siren is for a tsunami warning."

"Oh!" you reply, stunned. "I was wondering why everyone seemed to be hurrying away from the beach."

Turn the page.

Of course, it's not everyone. A few teenage boys are out on the exposed ocean floor, picking up rocks and shells. Others stand along the shoreline, gazing out at the horizon. The water isn't coming up—it's going down. Maybe that means it's safe. Besides, you can go have a quick look before any danger arrives. If there's a huge wave coming, you're sure to see it with plenty of time to get back up above the seawall here, right?

Max lets out a growl and a series of barks. He clearly doesn't want to go toward the sea. Does he know something that you don't?

To continue on and investigate the shore,
go to the next page.

To turn around and head for higher ground,
turn to page 16.

You've never seen anything like this before. You want to get some photos. You lead a reluctant Max down to the beach. It looks so strange to see so much of it exposed. The teenage boys are climbing on top of rocks that are usually a foot or two beneath the ocean surface.

"This is wild," you say to yourself as you wander farther out.

Crabs and other creatures scurry and slide along the sand. Normally, Max would be investigating all of it, but he just cowers near your feet. Suddenly, he lets out a loud yelp.

That's when one of the boys screams. Suddenly, all three of them are running back up the beach. Should you follow them?

To run back toward shore, turn to page 22.

To stay and watch the action, turn to page 34.

You remember watching a documentary on tsunamis. This is what happens before the wave hits. The water recedes as the wave approaches.

"I think you might be right about this one, Max," you say. "Let's get somewhere safer."

A few hundred feet ahead of you, there's a small building that serves as a public restroom and changing area. It stands at least 10 feet above the normal water level. The roof is probably high enough.

You keep scanning. A two-lane highway runs along the coast. On the other side of it, the land rises into a wooded area. You could cross the highway and head that way to get to even higher ground. But climbing through the woods doesn't seem like the smartest idea either.

You look again out to the ocean. Far off, near the horizon, you think you see a line. Is it your imagination, or is that a wave coming in? If so, you need to act quickly.

To cross the highway to reach higher ground, turn to page 18.

To head to the building, turn to page 23.

One last glance at the building tells you that if this is a major tsunami, you may need to get higher than that.

"Come on, boy," you urge Max, turning toward the highway.

A few other people have the same idea. The highway is busy, and there's no crosswalk here. Half a dozen people are waiting for a chance to cross.

As cars buzz by, you hear shouting from behind you. A glance over your shoulder tells you all you need to know. A large swell of water is clearly visible beyond the shore. The wave will be here before long.

"We can't wait," says a middle-aged man. He's dressed like he was out for a run.

The man steps out onto the road and puts out his hands. The cars in each direction slow down as people dart across the pavement. One woman even pulls her car over and joins you as you rush to higher ground.

Max barks as the two of you run up the rough ground. Behind you, people are screaming. The wave is here. The water level rises rapidly as it pushes inland. Within seconds, the beach is entirely covered. Moments later, water is spilling over the seawall.

"It's coming!" you shout. A few people have fallen behind, but the runner is still by your side, as well as the woman who left her car.

The water is over the seawall now, pushing inland with incredible force. Benches are swept away. Streetlights creak and bend under the force.

"Keep running!" shouts the woman.

The wooded area is just a few dozen feet ahead. The slope here remains gradual. But every step you take brings you farther from the sea and a little higher up. Will it be enough?

Turn the page.

To your right, stands a medium-sized oak tree. You could climb it to get out of the danger zone and ride out the disaster there. You could easily carry Max up with you.

To continue into the woods, go to the next page.

To climb the tree, turn to page 27.

Will a tree even be strong enough to withstand the wave? You're not sure, so you keep running.

The water is coming fast. Already, you can see it washing over the lower-lying land to your left. The man in the running gear has pulled ahead of you and disappeared into the trees, but the woman from the car is right behind you.

Suddenly, you hear her scream. You glance over your shoulder and see that she's fallen. Water is rushing toward both of you. In a moment of confusion, you let go of Max's leash. He darts off into the woods as fast as his legs can carry him.

To go after Max, turn to page 30.

To help the woman, turn to page 31.

Something scared those boys. A quick glance out to sea confirms it—a wave is coming. There isn't much time.

"Run, Max!" you shout.

Together, the two of you sprint over the wet sand toward dry shore. You can't get far before the raging, monstrous wave reaches you. It seems to have popped up out of the blue. But there's a building ahead—a public restroom and changing area. It stands about 10 feet above the normal sea level. It might just be enough—if you can get there in time.

Go to the next page.

Your heart races as you sprint the final few feet toward the building. It's a single-story wooden building with a cement foundation. A dozen or so other people are standing on the cement platform, looking out at the water. They're huddled between the building and the beach below.

Turn the page.

The wave hits just as you bound up a few stairs to the slab. The seawall holds back the water for now, but as the water swells, it climbs higher and higher up the wall. A young girl is screaming as she watches the churning water coming closer and closer. Max starts barking. Nearby, people scream in terror. But all of that noise is almost drowned out by the roar of the water as it swallows up the shore.

Some of the people gathered are running inside the building for shelter. Part of you wants to join them. But you're not sure it's high enough. A dumpster sits alongside the wall of the building. You might be able to use it to climb onto the roof.

To try to get on the roof, go to the next page.

To take shelter inside, turn to page 36.

You're too low here. The water is going to reach you in seconds.

"Follow me," you shout to anyone listening.

You scoop Max up under one arm and use the other to leap on top of the dumpster. From there, you grab onto a bracket that holds a metal gutter along the roofline. You hoist up Max, then pull yourself up. You scrape your leg on the sharp gutter but ignore the pain.

Once you're on the roof, you spin around. Only two people have followed you—the crying girl and a woman you assume is her mother. The girl is climbing onto the dumpster now with the woman's help.

"Grab my hand," you tell her.

The girl reaches up. You stretch as far as you can and barely grab hold. It takes all of your strength to haul her up and over the roofline.

Turn the page.

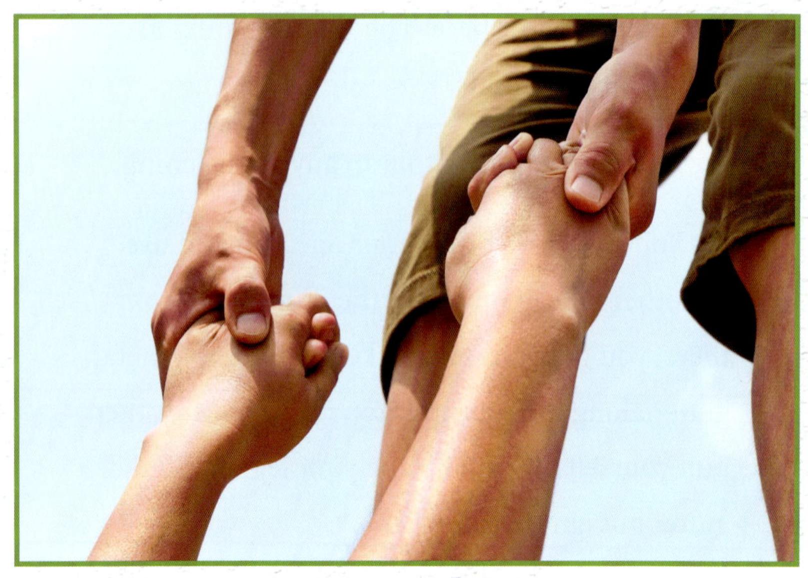

"Mom!" cries the girl, pointing.

On the ground, her mother is trying to climb onto the dumpster as water rushes past. It's up to her ankles . . . her shins. She can't make the leap without your help . . . but going back down will put you right back in harm's way.

To tell her how to get up on her own, turn to page 39.

To jump down to help, turn to page 41.

The slope is too gradual. You can hear the tsunami rolling in behind you. The sound of the rushing water almost drowns out the honking cars and screaming people.

"The tree!" you shout. The man and woman either don't hear you or ignore you. They're going to run for it. You dart for the tree.

You used to climb trees all the time as a kid, and this one is perfect. You scoop Max up under your arm and hoist yourself up onto the low branch. From there, you're able to climb from branch to branch until you're at least 20 feet up. Max is barking nonstop now. You don't even try to quiet him.

The water surges below you, flooding the ground. Debris that looks like part of a building crashes into the base of the tree before breaking up and washing farther inland.

Turn the page.

The tree creaks and sways. If it breaks, you're dead. But this is an oak. If any tree is strong enough to stand up to the power of a tsunami, this should be it.

Minutes of chaos and terror pass as you cling to the trunk. The water reaches the lowest branch. It churns below you like an endless river, carrying

everything it has gathered along the way. You watch as a car is dragged across the ground you just covered. In the distance, the roof of a small building collapses into the rushing water. You can't imagine how you would survive if you got swept up in that.

The minutes feel like hours. The first wave was the biggest, but several more follow it. The water churns and surges below the tree, but the sturdy oak holds strong.

After what feels like forever, the water returns to the ocean for good. You and Max make your way down onto the ground. Everything is soaking wet, and debris is everywhere.

"Come on, Max," you say, pointing toward the woods. "We need to see if the others made it."

THE END

To follow another path, turn to page 8.
To learn more about tsunamis, turn to page 97.

You can't lose Max!

"Max!" you call out.

You charge after your dog. But your foot catches a tree root. You fall head over heels onto the ground. Your head hits a sharp rock.

You're dazed for just a moment. But it's a moment you didn't have to spare. A churning wall of water slams into you. It spins you around and drags you in an irresistible current. You fight to keep your head above the water, but it's hopeless. Time and time again, you're dragged under.

Finally, a large piece of debris slams into you. The world goes dark. You slip under the surging water once again. This time, you won't be coming back up. You hope Max fared better.

THE END

To follow another path, turn to page 8.
To learn more about tsunamis, turn to page 97.

Max is fast, and the woman needs help. You take a few steps back and reach out your arm.

"I twisted my ankle," she says.

You can barely hear her over the noise and chaos around you. You shake your head and grab her hand.

"You have to run or you're dead," you say, pulling her to her feet.

To your relief, she can still run, and you help her along. You spot a high point—a cluster of rocks along the base of some trees. You both move as fast as you can. Tree branches smack you in the face, but you don't slow down.

The water reaches you just as you leap onto the rocks. You grab a tree trunk and hold on. So does the woman. This might be the end.

But it's not. You knew that if you could get high enough, the wave wouldn't reach you.

Turn the page.

You got exactly that high. A series of waves pushes the water farther and farther in. It gets terrifyingly close, but it never makes it to your perch on the rocks. You watch with relief as the waves recede and don't come back.

The woman clings to a tree nearby.

"Is it over?" she asks.

You look around at the debris piled all along the shore. The waterline is back to it's original point. You're pretty sure the tsunami is over. Just then, you hear an excited bark behind you. You turn to see Max—with the runner.

"Look who I found," he says with a grin as he hands you Max's leash.

All four of you are unharmed. But you know that many weren't so lucky.

"Come on, let's start back," you say. "There may be people who need our help."

THE END

To follow another path, turn to page 8.
To learn more about tsunamis, turn to page 97.

"Everyone is acting so crazy," you tell Max with a laugh. "What are they so afraid of?"

That's when you hear a huge wave rushing to shore. A white-capped line of water is bearing down on you at a speed that's almost hard to comprehend. That's what sent the boys running for shore.

It's a tsunami, and you're in the worst place you can be. You drop Max's leash.

"Run!" you shout to the little dog.

Max takes off as fast as he can. So do you. But it's hopeless. There's no high ground close enough. Before you know it, the powerful wave is upon you.

The surge slams into you with shocking force. Your body is tossed and dragged against the rocky seafloor as the huge wave plows over everything in its path.

In some ways, you're lucky. The force of the wave knocked you unconscious from the start. You never stood a chance, but you also didn't have to suffer. You're a victim of one of nature's most violent outbursts and your own bad decision.

THE END

To follow another path, turn to page 8.
To learn more about tsunamis, turn to page 97.

Maybe the walls of the building will protect you from the powerful wave.

"Everyone, inside!" you shout.

You push open the wooden door, which leads to a small hallway. Men's and women's changing rooms stand to each side. You and Max lead the way in, and several others follow you. You slam the door shut and lock it.

But the water rushes in under the door. As the sea level outside rises, the wave shatters windows and pours into the building. You climb onto a bench that sits along the hallway. But the water keeps rising. Within moments, it's at your feet again. The lights in the building flicker out.

As the wave outside grows, something large slams into the building. The door crashes in.

Water sweeps the bench out from under your feet. Suddenly, you're waist-deep in the brackish current, and you've lost Max.

Turn the page.

The door is the only way out, and the force of the water flowing in makes it impossible to reach.

The rising water isn't going to stop anytime soon. You're trapped. You gasp for breath as the water rises over your head. It is the last breath you take. Your final thought is that you wish you had climbed onto the roof.

THE END

To follow another path, turn to page 8.
To learn more about tsunamis, turn to page 97.

"Grab this bracket and pull yourself up!" you shout. "You can do it!"

All around you, the powerful wave sweeps away everything in its path. The woman tries one last time to climb atop the dumpster. She's almost there when the water washes her away.

From the rooftop, you watch a nightmare unfold all around you. The tsunami sweeps over the land with unstoppable force. The building below you creaks and groans. It could collapse at any moment.

Somehow, it doesn't. The water rises more than halfway up the height of the building. There are screams from every direction. Sirens wail in the distance. And the constant rush of water, as more waves follow the first, seems to swallow up the land. After what feels like hours, the water finally begins to recede. It carries so much trash and debris.

Turn the page.

You try not to look too closely at everything in that current. You know there are bodies in there. The waves swell and retreat several times before the sea evens out again. But the world around you is a totally different landscape. Buildings have crumbled. Splintered wood beams, garbage, bikes, and even vehicles are scattered about. The dumpster you climbed up on has long since floated away.

Hours later, a helicopter rescues you and the little girl. You close your eyes as the helicopter takes you to an inland hospital. All you can see is the face of her mother, struggling to get to the roof. Should you have done more? That question will haunt you for the rest of your life.

THE END

To follow another path, turn to page 8.
To learn more about tsunamis, turn to page 97.

If you don't help her, this woman will die. With a deep breath, you leap back down onto the dumpster. In one motion, you grab the woman under the arms and drag her up onto the dumpster.

You can feel the dumpster shifting and moving under your feet as the water swells. It's chained to the wall, but that won't hold long.

"Grab the bracket," you shout.

The woman does. She pulls herself up with as much strength as she can muster, while you push her up from below.

There's no time to waste. You reach for the bracket, but as you do, rushing water tears the dumpster from its chains. In a heartbeat, you're thrown into the rushing water. You swim for the surface, trying to keep your head above water. You're being washed inland, along with everything else the wave touches.

Turn the page.

In a stroke of luck, you spot a large foam beach cushion among the debris. You grab on and float with it.

The next several minutes are a battle for your life. The water drags you along, trying its best to suck you under. But the beach cushion is just enough to keep you afloat. You cling to it with every bit of strength you have.

Finally, you catch a break. The current drags you past a low-hanging tree branch. You grab on and pull yourself out of the water. You sit on the branch exhausted but alive. You know that in time, the water will recede. Rescue will come. All you can do for now is hang on. You think about the mother and the little girl. You hope the building was high enough and that it withstood the strength of the monstrous tsunami.

THE END

To follow another path, turn to page 8.
To learn more about tsunamis, turn to page 97.

CHAPTER 3

MAKING WAVES

You had spent the morning on your small fishing boat, and you were taking your catch to the market to sell when the siren went off. Your best friend, Ahmed, is with you.

"Tsunami!" you and Ahmed shout together.

This part of the island is low-lying. It's the worst place to be if a tsunami is coming.

"Leave the fish," Ahmed tells you. "My house is in a safe place. Let's get there before the wave hits."

Turn the page.

You're not so sure. Ahmed lives miles from here, and the streets will be jam-packed with people trying to flee. You could be back to your boat in a minute or two and out into deep water within five minutes. In deep water, your boat will barely even feel the tsunami. It's not until the wave reaches shallow areas that it rises and becomes a problem. Besides, the idea of leaving your catch behind is hard enough to swallow, much less leaving your boat docked. The wave will destroy it.

People are rushing past you in both directions. Merchants are quickly packing up their stalls. The siren continues to blare.

Ahmed is impatient. Should you go with him or go back to the boat? He has a wife and a young son at home. He'll never agree to go to the boat.

To go with Ahmed and try to get to high ground, go to the next page.

To return to your boat and head for deep water, turn to page 48.

Ahmed is right. It's smarter to get to higher ground than to return to the boat. You set down the basket and take off running with him.

Ahmed's house is a few miles away, and it's all along low-lying terrain. You hope you can get there before the tsunami hits.

A thought pops up into your head. Ahmed works as a mechanic at a motorcycle shop. The shop sits in the opposite direction, though—right along the shoreline. If you risk going in a more dangerous direction, it could pay off if you get a pair of motorcycles to make your escape.

To continue on foot toward Ahmed's house, turn to page 53.

To suggest the motorcycle shop, turn to page 55.

"Get to your family, Ahmed. I'm taking my boat out to sea."

Ahmed looks at you like you've gone crazy.

"Out to sea? Why would you go to your boat in a tsunami warning?"

"Tsunamis are only big where it's shallow. I can get out to deep water where it's safer. Get to your family, and I'll see you when this is over."

With that, you hurry back toward your boat, working against a flow of people heading the opposite way. Finally, you reach the small boat, untie it, and fire up the little motor.

Most of the boats here are hurrying to shore. It's only you and a few others headed out. You speed along the narrow channel that leads into the bay. Within minutes, you're out into the open sea. You know the ocean floor drops deeply about a mile offshore. You need to get there to be safe from the worst of the wave.

As you motor along, you notice another small boat bobbing in the water ahead. You feel compelled to help the man driving it. You veer in the direction of the boat. The man sees you coming and waves his arms.

"It won't start," he says desperately. "I think it's low on gas. Do you have any to spare?"

Turn the page.

You do have an emergency gas can, but there's no time to spare.

"Forget it," you call, pulling your boat alongside his. "Just get in. We have to get to deep water now."

The man recoils. "Leave my boat! Never! Now if you could just find some gas . . ."

You can feel a rush of warmth to your face as anger rises up in you. You're risking your life to help this man, and he's putting both your lives at risk. Every second you spend here increases the danger. How far are you willing to go?

To lie and tell him you don't have extra gas, go to the next page.

To give in and find your spare gas can, turn to page 59.

"I don't have any extra gas," you lie. "Are you getting in or not?"

The man just scowls at you and goes back to trying to start his motor. You won't risk your life for this stubborn man. You open the throttle all the way and speed away from shore. A small wave hits before you reach deep water, but you know that tsunamis often have more than one wave, and the first one isn't always the biggest.

The boat skips over the small waves, leaving a wake behind. You can tell by the darkening blue of the water that you're moving into deeper water.

You slowly pull back on the throttle, until you're moving just enough to control your heading. You don't need to go out any farther, but you want to keep pointed out to sea. That way when the wave comes, you'll hit it head-on. That's the safest way to take on any big wave.

Turn the page.

A minute later, another tsunami wave passes. At first, you're not even sure it happened. Out here, it's nothing but a gradual rise in the water. But you watch it after it passes. Once it hits shallower water, it grows. From out here you can see the wave tossing boats around like toys. Moments later, the water surges onto the land. The coastline itself seems to disappear as the water swallows everything in its path.

You can only imagine the chaos there right now. It would probably be safest for you to stay here for a few hours as the tragedy passes. It looks like this was the big wave, but there could still be more coming. On the other hand, if you head back in, maybe you could be helpful.

To wait out the tsunami here, turn to page 62.

To go in to help rescue survivors, turn to page 63.

Heading to the motorcycle shop means going toward the ocean—something you do not want to do. The two of you press on, weaving through cars and people in the busy city streets.

Cars are lined up bumper-to-bumper. Nobody is moving. People clog the sidewalks. You've barely moved a block when the tsunami hits.

Turn the page.

Over your shoulder, you see a wall of water rolling over everything. Boats in the marina—including yours—are tossed and turned like toys. The beach has disappeared. The water surges up the street, covering your feet, your ankles, your knees. The current is strong. Already, you can feel your footing slipping.

There's a fire escape on a three-story building to one side of you. You could reach it, but Ahmed is already a few dozen feet in front of you. Taking that escape means splitting up. Are you willing to do that?

To try to stick with Ahmed, turn to page 58.

To climb the fire escape, turn to page 67.

"Ahmed!" you shout. "Your shop isn't far from here. We can make it a lot faster on wheels."

Ahmed hesitates. He's not supposed to take the shop's bikes out. But if there's a wave coming, they would be ruined there anyway.

"OK," he finally agrees.

It takes a few minutes to reach the shop. Ahmed unlocks the garage, and you find a couple of dirt bikes. Their engines rev a high-pitched wail as you take them out.

Turn the page.

The streets are gridlocked with traffic. Everyone is trying to flee the tsunami. But the little dirt bikes are small and agile. The two of you weave through traffic.

You're just a few blocks from shore when the wave hits. The tsunami is huge. You can hear the rushing water and the crashing and snapping of wood and debris as it slams into everything in its path.

"Gun it!" you shout.

Up until now, you've been carefully weaving through traffic. But now you have to go. You squeeze the throttle and grip the handlebars. Ahmed is a skilled rider. He scoots up onto a sidewalk, over a loading ramp, then across a section of road. Behind you, the wave is pushing forward. Cars are being swept away. People are screaming. Buildings are creaking and cracking under the stress.

You're still too slow, and too many people crowd the streets. You're not going to make it.

Then you spot a section of road that is closed for construction. It leads to an inland hill—and there's nobody on it.

"That way," you shout and lead the way.

The wave is less than a block behind you as you reach the open section of road. You crank the throttle wide open. The motor sings as you rocket down the street—gaining both distance and a bit of elevation with every passing block.

It's just enough. The wave finally loses its strength. You stop and watch as the first wave slowly recedes.

"Come on, let's get to your family," you say. Ahmed gives you a nod, and you're off again.

Turn to page 65.

You're not going to abandon Ahmed. You do your best to catch up to him, sloshing through the rapidly rising water. The force is surprising. It's knocking people over. One misstep will send you over as well.

Ahmed charges toward a small city park ahead. The land rises along a low ridge there. You manage to make it without slipping into the surge of water. Dry land has never felt so good.

"Come on," Ahmed shouts, pointing ahead. "This ridge runs all way to my house."

You follow him. The water continues to rise amidst the chaos around you, but the ridge is high enough to remain dry. The wave tips cars and collapses buildings. Ahead, a fire burns—probably from a gas leak. But you stay just high enough above the churning water. Soon, Ahmed's house is in sight.

Turn to page 65.

"Hold on!" you shout. You reach down and find your emergency gas can.

"There's not a lot there, but it should be enough to get you started," you say as you hand the can over. The man grabs it and leans over his motor. He carefully pulls out a dented metal funnel and slowly pours the gas into the small tank.

"Hurry up," you call with impatience.

The man taps the can onto the funnel a few times, trying to get every last drop. Then he screws the top back on and sets it down, while he again tries to pull-start the motor.

This is taking too long. You don't care if you get the gas can back anymore. You need to go, so you open up the throttle and start back out. You don't get far before a line of blue-black water is bearing down on you.

Turn the page.

As the wave hits shallow water, it rises rapidly. By the time it reaches your boat, it's a wall of water. You never had a chance. The tsunami slams into you. Within seconds, your boat tips over, throwing you into the surging sea. The water drags you down . . . down . . . down.

THE END

To follow another path, turn to page 8.
To learn more about tsunamis, turn to page 97.

You can't be sure that the worst is over. What if there are more waves coming? The best thing you can do is keep yourself safe.

From out here, it's hard to gauge the devastation. You can see boats littered along the coast. Eventually, you decide it's safe to head back. The water is filled with debris. You try not to look too closely at it, fearing that there might be bodies. You know many people must have lost their lives.

When you reach land, you're sickened by what you see. The entire town is flattened. There are dead and injured people scattered all over. Everywhere you look, people are crying out in pain and trauma. You can't help but wonder if you could have helped someone if you had come back sooner. The guilt will stick with you for life.

THE END

To follow another path, turn to page 8.
To learn more about tsunamis, turn to page 97.

You're pretty sure the worst has passed. You should be safe now. But others must be fighting for their lives. Maybe you can help.

You turn your boat toward shore and carefully head back in. As you move, you scan the surface of the water. Debris floats everywhere. The tsunami has wrecked boats, ruined buildings, and picked up everything that wasn't tied down. Now much of that stuff is drifting out to sea. You don't want to hit any of it.

After a few minutes, you spot something moving in the water. As you draw closer, you see it's a person—and they're alive! You pull alongside the person and toss them a life vest. It's a young girl. She looks exhausted.

"Give me your hand!" you call.

Weakly, she reaches out. When you grab her hand, her skin is so cold.

Turn the page.

You haul up the girl. She collapses into the boat. You give her a small blanket from your storage trunk.

"Thank you," she says. Her voice is barely a whisper. "My family . . . they could be out here too."

"We'll keep looking," you promise. You can probably fit eight people in this boat. You've saved one life already. You're not going to stop until you've done all you can to save more.

THE END

To follow another path, turn to page 8.
To learn more about tsunamis, turn to page 97.

When you reach Ahmed's house, you're in luck. The small one-story house sits on a rocky ridge that overlooks the ocean.

"Thank goodness," Ahmed gasps as he bursts through the front door. "I didn't think the wave would get here, but I was still worried."

The two of you go in to find Ahmed's family. They watched it all from the roof just in case the water got too high.

"I'm afraid my boat and my house are gone," you say, sadly.

You live close to the water in a neighborhood where everything has likely been wiped out. You fear for your neighbors. It will take months or years of rebuilding. You've lost everything.

"You can stay with us as long as you need," Ahmed says.

Turn the page.

Tomorrow, you'll head down to see if your boat and house are still there. You expect that everything you own is gone. But at least you have a place to stay and friends who are willing to help when you need it the most.

THE END

To follow another path, turn to page 8.
To learn more about tsunamis, turn to page 97.

Ahmed is faster than you. He's already outrunning you. You have to get to safety. You leap for the fire escape, grabbing the bottom rung with all your strength. You pull yourself up out of the rushing water. It's rising by the second, raging through the city, carrying away everything in its path.

You haul yourself up onto the roof of the building. There are a dozen other people already there. Together, you watch in horror as the wave sweeps through the city. Some buildings crumble. You watch an entire roof float past the one you're standing on.

"We're trapped," says a woman. "It will be days before help comes."

You shake your head.

"It might take a while before the water recedes, but it won't be days," you say. "We just have to sit tight until it's safe to go back down."

Turn the page.

After a few hours, the water has mostly receded. It leaves a devastated wasteland behind. Debris litters the streets. Entire buildings have collapsed. Thousands are dead. It's a nightmare.

In time, rescue workers bring you to shelter in camps. There are so many homeless now. There's little food and clean water. Disease spreads through the crowded camps.

Every day, you hope to see Ahmed again. But you never do. He, like so many others, became a victim of nature's fury. You'll always wonder what happened to him. You hope he didn't come back looking for you and got swept up in the wave.

THE END

To follow another path, turn to page 8.
To learn more about tsunamis, turn to page 97.

CHAPTER 4

TO THE RESCUE

You know exactly what the siren means—a tsunami is coming. You're a police officer, trained to help others in exactly this kind of situation. You had biked to the beach on your day off, but now you hop back on it and ride as fast as you can to the police station. It's a couple miles inland and uphill, safe from the tsunami waves that batter the coastlines. Disaster is coming, and people are going to need your help.

Turn the page.

The first wave of the tsunami hits while you're biking to the station, but you're well ahead of it. When you get there, alarms wail throughout the building. Andrea, the police chief, stands in front of a small briefing room. She confirms that a tsunami has hit, and she barks out orders. Several dozen firefighters gather, along with paramedics and police officers.

“We’ve got damage all along the coast,” Andrea says as all the voices suddenly quiet. “The waves have reached almost a mile inland in places. Along the riverbeds, it’s even worse. We’ve got property damage everywhere. There are fires from gas leaks. Buildings near the coast have collapsed from the strength of the wave. But today, property damage is not our concern. This is a full-blown rescue effort. People are dying out there. We need to rescue everyone we can reach.”

The tsunami struck with little warning, giving people precious minutes to find safety. You’re lucky you thought as quickly as you did. As a police officer, you’ve been trained in medical rescues, and, as a former U.S. Marine, you’re well prepared to face any situation. You’re eager to get out there and start saving lives. You give a nod to your partner, Hank. You know he feels the same way.

Turn the page.

“Okay, everyone. Get out there and help people,” Andrea says. “Be safe but remember that they’re counting on us. This is what we’ve trained for. Now let’s do it.”

You and Hank quickly head to the roof where a rescue helicopter is waiting. As the chopper takes off, you look down at the landscape below. You can barely believe what you see. There’s water everywhere. Smoke rises from burning buildings. Boats have been washed blocks inland. Structures have collapsed.

The chopper banks hard to the right. To one side is the city, while a heavily wooded state park lies to the other. Reports are coming over the radio. Hank is listening carefully, jotting down notes.

“We’ve got a report of campers stranded in the state park, clinging to fallen trees as the water rushes all around them. Another report has a group stranded on the rooftop of a building near one of the fires.”

Your mind races. The campers might be in the more immediate danger. But reaching them could be hard. Should you try it, or head for the people stranded on the rooftop?

To head for the campers, turn to page 76.

To make your way to the rooftop, turn to page 77.

“Those campers won’t last long. We’ve got to save them,” you shout. Hank nods and tells the pilot where to go.

A large river empties into the ocean in the middle of the park. The wave ran up the river and overflowed its banks—right where the park’s campgrounds lie. As the chopper soars in, you can see the danger. A family of four is clinging to some strong oak trees. Everything around them is flooded, and they’re barely hanging on against the relentless current. You must act fast.

To go down in a rescue basket, turn to page 78.

To toss the family life vests, turn to page 84.

The people stuck on the roof are nearby, and you're sure you can help them.

"Let's get those people stuck on the rooftop," you tell Hank.

The helicopter banks to the left, soaring over the ruined city below. As you approach, you realize that the situation is more complex than you thought. There are three people on a roof next to a building that is going up in flames. And there are five on the building that's burning. Flames burn on two sides of the building, and a plume of smoke rises into the sky.

"Which building?" Hank asks.

The group of three should be easy to save. The group of five will be much harder. You'll be putting yourself, Hank, and the pilot at risk. And to make matters worse, the helicopter can only carry seven people—with the three of you included, you can't carry all five.

To go to the burning building, turn to page 80.

To save the group of three, turn to page 86.

Life vests won't do these people much good if debris hits them. They need to be rescued.

"I'm going down," you tell Hank. The helicopter's rescue basket is designed to hold one person, but you hook into a second line and go down alongside it.

First, you go to a teenage girl. The water is rushing above her knees. You quickly wrap a strap under her arms and help her into the metal basket. She's shaking. Hank brings her up, unloads her quickly, then lowers the basket back down.

You quickly save the next two people—a man and a young boy. A woman remains. She's clinging to a large oak, and there's no way for you to get the basket to her. Your safest option is to toss her a line. She would have to fight her way through the surging water, but you're not sure she has the strength. The other option is to go get her. You would have to unclip yourself from the helicopter, putting you at the mercy of the water.

To toss a line to the woman, turn to page 82.

To unclip and go to her, turn to page 88.

“Those people need to get off that building now,” you tell Hank. “We’ve got to get them first.”

As the helicopter descends through the black smoke, you realize how dangerous the situation is. The fire is burning hot, and there’s no telling how long the rooftop will hold. If it collapses, it will be a disaster.

The helicopter hovers about 12 feet over the rooftop, and you drop a ladder. You quickly climb down and step off as the people hurry to you. They’re on the verge of panic, and you need to calm them down.

“Just hold tight and climb. We have to hurry,” you tell them.

You send them up one by one. After the fourth person reaches the helicopter, you know that there’s only room for one more. A middle-aged man stands beside you.

“Go,” you tell him. “The helicopter will get you to a safe place and come back for me.”

The man thanks you and scrambles up the ladder. Hank looks down at you and gives you a nod.

"We'll get back as quickly as we can, hold tight," he shouts.

With that, the helicopter is off. You stand alone on the rooftop. The fire is spreading rapidly. From below, you hear a loud crash as part of an outer wall collapses.

Another building stands near the one you're on. A gap of about 7 feet separates the two buildings. Could you make the leap? You're not sure. And if you don't make the jump, it's certain death. But then, staying here might mean the same thing.

To attempt the jump, turn to page 90.

To wait here for the helicopter, turn to page 93.

You can't help anyone if you get swept up in the water.

"Catch this," you shout over the noisy hum of the helicopter. You wait until the woman nods, then toss the line. Luckily, it's a perfect throw, and she grabs it without having to let go of the tree trunk. The woman wraps the line around her waist and nods again.

"I'm ready," she says.

"Just hold on tight," you shout back.

The woman lets go and drops down into the rushing water. The line goes instantly tight as the current carries her. You slowly reel her in as she fights the current. In a few moments, you have her. You give Hank a thumbs-up, and he carefully pulls you up.

The two of you check over all four survivors. No one is seriously hurt. With the helicopter full, you head back to base to drop them off.

"We can never thank you enough!" says the man.

He and his family were sure they were going to die. It feels good to know that you made a difference, but there are plenty more people out there who need you. You and Hank head back out to help.

THE END

To follow another path, turn to page 8.
To learn more about tsunamis, turn to page 97.

You grab four bright orange life vests. The helicopter hovers low—just barely above the treetops.

"Here, take these!" you shout.

You toss the vests one by one toward the people. Only one of them actually catches a vest. In horror, you watch as the powerful current tears one of the people away from the tree. You catch sight of the camper briefly in the water, then they're gone.

"What are you doing!" Hank shouts.

"Lower the basket!" Hank tells the pilot as he clips himself into a line alongside the small metal rescue basket.

You watch as Hank goes to each person and brings them up in the safety of the basket one by one. He and the three victims are slowly pulled up.

They are all in shock, with tears streaming down their faces. They had to watch their beloved family member be swept away, and you know it was your fault.

You'll keep working. You'll try to do better. But you'll never be able to forgive yourself for failing this family.

THE END

To follow another path, turn to page 8.
To learn more about tsunamis, turn to page 97.

There are three people that you know you can rescue.

"Let's get them out of here," you say. "Then I'll come back on my own for the other five."

The helicopter lowers itself to just a few feet above the rooftop. You and Hank both hop off and rush to the terrified people.

"Let's go!" you tell them as you rush them up the ladder to the chopper.

There's no telling when that fire might spread to this building. You want to get these people to safety as soon as possible and come back for the others.

You and Hank help all three up and into the helicopter. Within minutes, you're off, headed back to the station to take them to safety.

When you return, the plume of smoke over the burning building is three times bigger. You can't even see the rooftop through the think blackness.

"There's too much smoke," Hank says sadly. "We can't help them."

Suddenly, the building sways and crumbles. The helicopter slowly lifts away. You can't take your eyes off the falling building. Those people are doomed. There's nothing you can do now.

You saved three people. But was it the right choice? You know that question will haunt you for the rest of your life.

THE END

To follow another path, turn to page 8.

To learn more about tsunamis, turn to page 97.

What if the woman is too weak to catch the line? What if your throw misses her and causes her to lose her grip? You couldn't live with yourself.

With a deep breath, you unclip yourself and drop into the water. It's deeper than you expect, and the current pulls on you instantly. You fight through it and slosh over to the tree she's holding.

"I've got you," you promise as she lets go of the tree and grabs onto you.

The strength of the moving water makes the walk back difficult. Already, you're both getting tired. But you make it somehow. You use all of your strength to help her up into the rescue basket, which hovers a few feet above the water.

You try to haul yourself up next. Your clothes are soaked, and your hands are wet. You can't get a good grip. The woman tries to help by pulling you, but she has no strength left.

You take a breath and prepare for another try. But at that moment, one of the nearby trees comes crashing down. It clips the basket, causing it to lurch toward you. The corner of the basket slams into your head. Suddenly, everything goes black. You slip into the water, unconscious.

Like every rescue worker, you willingly put your own life on the line to help others. At least you saved four lives before losing your own.

THE END

To follow another path, turn to page 8.
To learn more about tsunamis, turn to page 97.

The fire is spreading quickly. The smoke is getting thicker by the moment. Even if the building doesn't collapse, you're not sure the helicopter will be able to get to you through the heavy smoke.

You have to act. You take a running start and launch yourself into the air. It feels like slow motion as you soar between the buildings. Your jump comes up short, and your lower body slams hard into the brick edge of the second building. Something snaps in your leg, but you manage to grab onto the ledge.

Using every bit of your strength, you pull yourself up to the roof. You flop onto the rooftop and lay there. Terrible pain shoots through your leg. Moments later, the burning building collapses. If you'd stayed, you'd be dead.

You lay there for a moment, until a young man and woman approach you. "That was amazing," says the man. "Are you okay?"

In your hurry, you forgot that there were people on this roof as well. The woman helps you turn onto your back.

"That was incredible," she says, "But I'm pretty sure your leg is broken."

You grunt and nod—you knew that already. A few minutes later, the helicopter returns. Hank hurries down. He helps you up, along with the others on the roof.

Turn the page.

"What are you, some kind of action hero?" he jokes as you pull yourself up the ladder with your arms and one good leg.

You manage a small grin through the pain. A broken leg is a small price to pay to save five lives. You'll recover and be ready to help again the next time disaster strikes.

THE END

To follow another path, turn to page 8.
To learn more about tsunamis, turn to page 97.

Jumping would be a huge risk. You aren't sure you could make it. Your best bet is to wait and hope Hank makes it back before the fire spreads too far.

Seconds turn to minutes. The heat of the blaze leaves you dripping in sweat. The black smoke is everywhere. You pull your shirt over your face to try to filter out the air. But you're coughing and struggling to breathe.

Turn the page.

Suddenly, you hear a huge crash from beneath you. The whole building seems to sway. Time is running out.

Finally, you hear the sound of the helicopter returning. But the smoke is so thick that you can't see anything. All you can do is wait and hope.

But you've run out of time. The building shifts violently, tipping to one side and throwing you off your feet. A moment later, one entire side of the roof collapses. You never would have guessed that a tsunami would lead to death by fire.

THE END

To follow another path, turn to page 8.

To learn more about tsunamis, turn to page 97.

CHAPTER 5

UNDERSTANDING TSUNAMIS

People used to call tsunamis tidal waves. Many thought that the tides played a role in forming them. While tides can affect how high a tsunami reaches, they're not the cause. Writings dating back to ancient Greece identified the real cause—underwater earthquakes.

Earthquakes are caused by sudden shifts along faults in Earth's plates. Pressure builds up along these faults, and when that pressure finally releases, it creates an earthquake. Faults can shift from side to side, or they can slide up and down. Those up-and-down quakes tend to cause the biggest tsunamis.

When the land moves suddenly, the water above it is displaced, or moved. It creates a ripple—a tsunami. Other events, such as volcanoes, underwater landslides, and even asteroid strikes, can also create tsunamis. But earthquakes are by far the main culprit.

Out in the deep ocean, a tsunami is rarely a big event. As the wave travels through deep water, it just creates a small swell. But as the wave reaches shallow coastal areas, the wave's power is concentrated. The volume of the wave has nowhere to go but up.

That's a problem for any coastline the wave hits. Tsunamis push massive amounts of water. That water surges over the land. In big tsunamis, it can push miles inland.

One of the world's deadliest tsunamis happened in the Indian Ocean in 2004. The wave struck many countries, including Indonesia, India, and Thailand. More than 220,000 people died. Seven years later, an earthquake off the coast of Japan sent a devastating tsunami that killed close to 20,000 people and did billions of dollars in damage to coastal towns and cities.

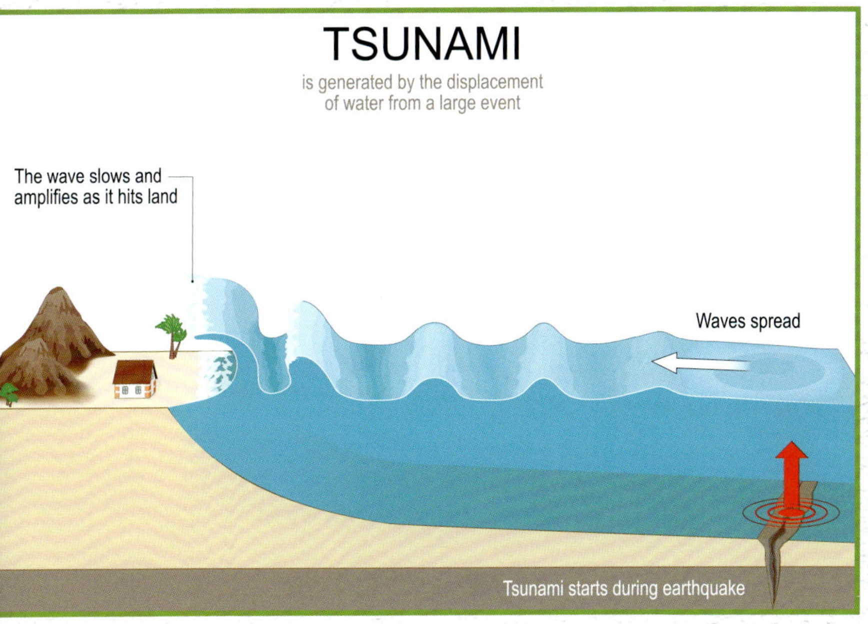

As populations continue to boom along coastlines all around the world, the danger of tsunamis only grows. They often come with little or no warning. Their pure power can be impossible to survive.

People can prepare by knowing where to go if a tsunami comes. Whether that's high ground nearby or the top of a sturdy building, quick action can be the difference between life and death.

TRUE TSUNAMI SURVIVAL STORIES

India, 2004

In 2004, a terrible tsunami struck coasts along the Indian Ocean. A young mother named Nazariah was home with her baby when the wave hit. She held on to the baby as the water swept them out of the house and into the streets.

Nazariah got lucky. The wave carried her past a police station. Officers pulled the two of them out of the water. They took shelter in the second story of the police station. But even that was not high enough. An officer had to break a hole in the ceiling so that they could all climb onto the roof.

Japan, 2011

The huge tsunami that hit Japan in 2011 caught many off guard. A man named Toru was working near the coast. He felt an earthquake and knew a wave could be coming. He rushed to his car to drive to high ground.

Toru got stuck in a traffic jam. He was in his car when the wave hit. It pushed him inland. Toru escaped out of his window, but the water still carried him along. He managed to grab onto the staircase of a building and pull himself to safety. He spent the night there with three other survivors, unable to help many others calling out for help.

Indonesia, 2018

Thirty-year-old Elis was taking a bath when a tsunami hit Indonesia in 2018. Elis was a mother with another child on the way. After the first, smaller, wave hit, Elis frantically tried to get dressed. That's when the second wave hit. It was much bigger. The wave slammed into the house, throwing debris everywhere. Some of it trapped Elis. She protected her unborn child as her husband worked to free her. Elis was battered and bruised, but she and the unborn baby were okay. Her child and parents had already fled.

TSUNAMI SURVIVAL KIT

Tsunamis can strike suddenly. One way to prepare is by having an emergency survival kit. A few basic items can give you a leg up when it comes to surviving a natural disaster.

backpack–to hold supplies

bottled water–at least 1 gallon (3.8 liters) per person

non-perishable food Don't forget a can opener!

flashlight and batteries

first aid kit containing
- bandages
- first aid creams
- alcohol/disinfectant wipes

toilet paper–Bring bags that can be sealed for bathroom waste.

sleeping bag/blankets

multi-tool

wrench and pliers

whistle–to signal for help and rescue

STAYING SAFE IN A TSUNAMI

A tsunami can bring devastation and death. The waves can destroy buildings, wash away cars, and kill people caught in their path. Take a few steps to stay safe!

Listen for Emergency Alerts

Listen to radio or tune in to television news for updates. Listen for warning sirens and be ready to act.

Get to High Ground

Low-lying coastal areas are at the greatest risk. Immediately get to high ground. If there is no high ground near, try for the highest floor or roof of a sturdy building.

Get to Deep Water

If you're on a boat, get to deep water. The waves won't have as big of an impact there.

Bring Supplies

Have an emergency kit ready. Food, water, and other supplies can help you get through the hours and days following a tsunami.

GLOSSARY

debris (duh-BREE)—scattered pieces left after something has been destroyed

earthquake (UHRTH-kwayk)—a sudden, violent shaking of the ground; earthquakes are caused by the shifting of Earth's crust

fault (FAWLT)—a crack in Earth's surface

recede (ri-SEED)—to move back and away from

rescue basket (RES-kyoo BASS-kuht)—a small platform that can be lowered from a helicopter to carry a person to safety

sea level (SEE LEV-uhl)—the average level of the surface of the ocean, used as a starting point from which to measure the height or depth of any place

seawall (SEE-wall)—a structure built parallel to the shore to block storm surges, tsunamis, and high tides from spilling into a populated area

surge (SURJ)—a sudden, powerful forward movement

throttle (THROT-uhl)—a lever or handle that controls the speed of an engine

READ MORE

Eaton, Maxwell, III. *Tsunami*. New York: Roaring Brook Press, 2024.

Foxe, Steve. *Deadly Natural Disasters*. North Mankato, MN: Capstone Press, 2024.

Taylor, Charlotte. *Terrible Tsunamis*. New York: Gareth Stevens Publishing, 2023.

Vale, Jenna. *Earthquakes: The Worst in History*. New York: Gareth Stevens Publishing, 2025.

INTERNET SITES

NASA Science: What Is a Tsunami?
spaceplace.nasa.gov/tsunami/en/

National Geographic Kids: Tsunami Facts
natgeokids.com/uk/discover/geography/physical-geography/tsunamis/

Ready Kids: Tsunamis
ready.gov/kids/disaster-facts/tsunamis

ABOUT THE AUTHOR

Matt Doeden is a freelance author and editor from Minnesota. He's written numerous children's books on sports, music, current events, the military, extreme survival, and much more. His book *It's Outta Here* was included on Bank Street's Best Books of the Year List in 2022. He lives in Minnesota with his wife and two children.